The Ultimate Spearfishing Almanac

YEAR

The Ultimate Spearfishing Almanac

Copyright © 2020 SpearoPress

All rights reserved.

CONTENTS

1	Introduction to using the Almanac	1
2	Example dive log record form	3
3	Dive log record forms in detail	6
4	Dive log record forms	11
5	Time to review	172

INTRODUCTION TO USING THE ALMANAC

The majority of spearfishermen use their local knowledge, checking wind, tides and weather prior to a dive, but are ultimately still crossing their fingers hoping for the fish to be there. More often than not fish life isn't as expected and you are left scratching your head, putting any success or failure down to luck.

Sometimes though, the stars align and a dive becomes a day to remember, a red letter day, good fish are everywhere you look and you think you have cracked it, only to be sorely disappointed and frustrated when you try to replicate the conditions, same tides, same location, only this time, no fish.

The truth of the matter is that fish behavior is influenced by factors far beyond the things most spearfishermen consider when selecting a time, and place, to go diving. As well as the obvious things like tides, everything from barometric pressure to lunar cycles can play a part in where fish will be or how they will behave. Each area or spot, will have a different combination of factors that makes it come alive, and many fish will behave, and be found, differently depending on a variety of factors.

If you can record, and understand, the various influences, and what they mean for a particular spot, species, or area, you will be able to look at the conditions that matter most ahead of every dive, enabling you to pick dive days or locations with the highest chances of success. Not only that but you'll know where to concentrate your efforts when you are in the water, will you be hunting free swimming fish, will they be holed up, or feeding in weed beds?

Keeping accurate records with sufficient information about spots, and their conditions is the only practical way to identify what factors play a part at what site and for what species. Many spearfishermen keep basic records only to look back at the end of the season to find that despite their best efforts there appears to be no reliable correlation between their records and the best fish or fish activity, leaving them frustrated and confused. In reality, more often than not, the information simply doesn't include enough specific information to draw a reliable conclusion.

That's where 'The Ultimate Spearfishing Almanac' comes in, with carefully laid out dive log record forms, designed to encourage spearfishermen to record the most essential data in a simple and repeatable way. Each twin page spread includes areas to record a multitude of conditions known to influence fish behavior, along with space for notes and even maps for marking and recording the hot spots you identify.

The Ultimate Spearfishing Almanac is designed to be completed directly into the book with a ball point pen, recording as much data as you can about the dive using the various headings in the dive log record forms. Over time you will build up a picture of how a spot performs under a variety of conditions. At any point you can look back through your records and identify common factors on the best days, helping you select the ideal conditions to dive any spot, increasing the likelihood of having a great dive as well as your chances of bagging that trophy fish.

Exactly how you use the book is up to you but each book contains enough space to record up to 80 dives, that's just over 1.5 dives a week, a full season for many spearfishermen. You could use a separate book for each dive spot, enabling you to build up a more detailed picture over a longer period of time. Or even record conditions on days you don't dive giving you a wider picture still. The more information you can gather, the better your understanding will become.

Over the next two pages is an example record form completed to give you an idea of the sort of information to record, but feel free to change things to suit your style, area and conditions, the most important thing is to keep frequent and consistent records. The more data you record, the more dialed in you will be to how different conditions affect different spots.

The following chapter includes a more in depth look at some of the sections included in the record forms and how they are thought to influence fish behavior.

EXAMPLE DIVE LOG RECORD FORM

Location:	Newtons Cove Weymouth	Coordinates/Mark:	Back Reef and Sand	
Date:	20/08/20	Start Time:	14:00	Finish Time:	19:00
Sun Rise:	06:06	Sun Set:	20:19	Moon Phase:	Waxing Crescent

Conditions

Overcast	Clear	Sunny	Intermittent	Raining	Storm
	X	X			
Air Temp	Wind Speed	Wind Direction	Barometric press	Rising	Falling
21	14mph	Southerly	1002.71	X	

Water Conditions

Depth/s	Visibility	Water Temp	Wave Height
4 - 8m	1 - 2m	18	0.5m
Current	Tidal State	Low Tide	High Tide
None	Low Slack Rising	13:28	20:54

Species Seen / Catch Report

Bass x 3 none caught
Mullet x 6 one caught 3lb 4oz

Fish Behavior / Notes

Bass lying in stringweed
Mullet freeswimming 1 - 2m

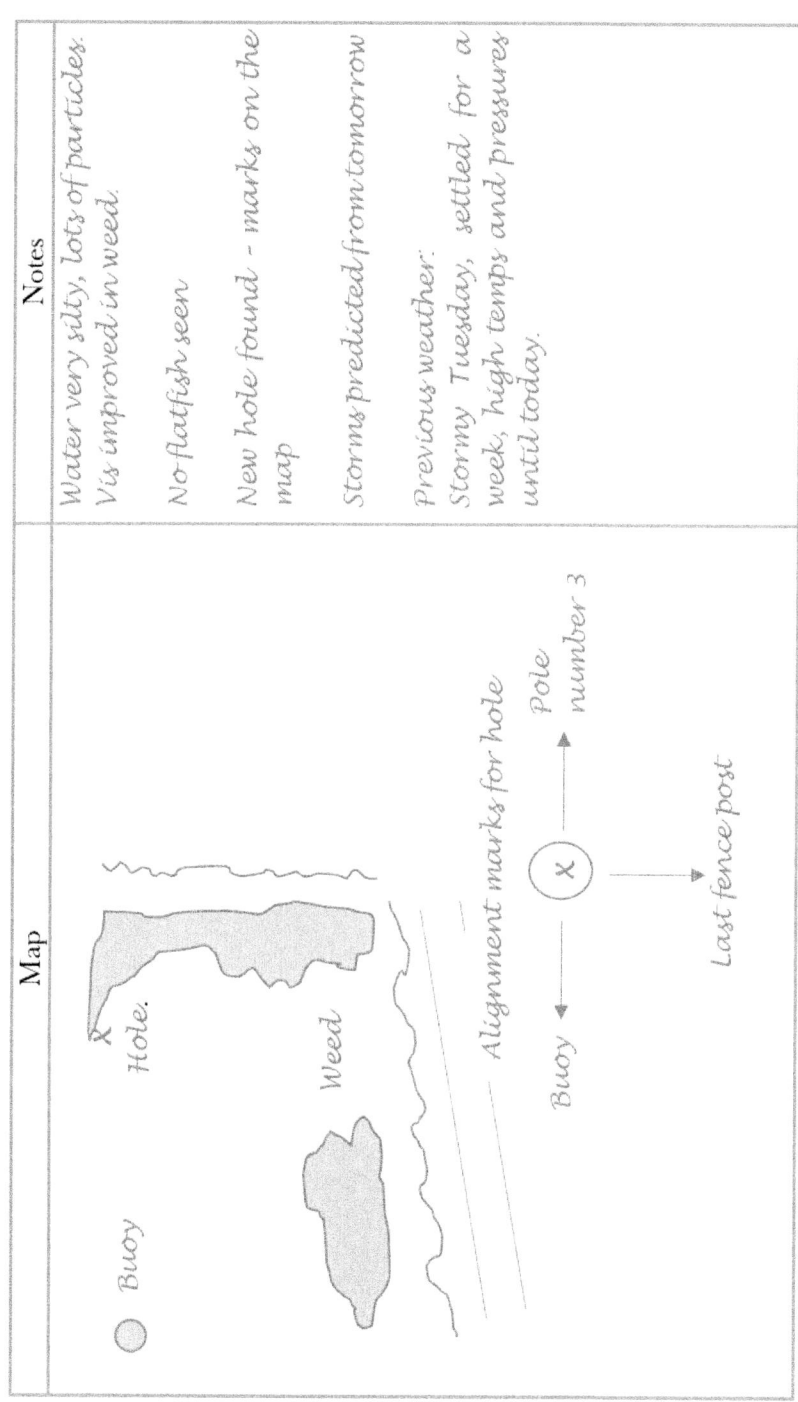

DIVE LOG RECORD FORMS IN DETAIL

This chapter covers some of the headings used in the record forms and how, or why, they may be important to fish behavior. Each fish species, and area is of course different but this overview will aid your understanding as well as introducing some factors you might not have considered before. Understanding each area of the record form and why it might be important to you and your particular spots and situation will help ensure you record the most pertinent data and that you learn the most from building up extensive records of your dives, sites and conditions.

Location.
Location should need no further explanation but its vital you can compare like for like when looking back months or even years in the future. Record your dive sites accurately, this might include indicating which end of the beach, which headland or specific spot you dived.

Coordinates/Marks.
Building from the last section, now is your opportunity to record any specific marks or hot spots in your dive site. A lot of spearfishing success is down to location; a particular hole, reef or structure could be the only point reliably holding fish in the entire area. With the availability of technology ever increasing, more and more divers are now using hand held GPS units, mobile phones or even watches to accurately mark positions. Not everyone of course is lucky enough to have access to such equipment, and what happens when that equipment fails? It's worth remembering that very accurate positioning can be achieved using the age-old technique of using land marks;

When in the water over your new hot spot look around to identify a feature or structure on the shoreline, that coincides or lines up with another, preferably much further away. For example, lining up the point of a headland with the spire of a church on the hill behind, the best landmarks to use are those that are permanent, stationary, and easily identified.

You can test a landmark's suitability by swimming left and right of your spot to see how the landmarks change in relation to each other, the bigger, and more noticeable the change, the more accurate your reference point will be.

This will give you a single reference point to work with but to accurately pin point your location you will need a second, preferably at 90 degrees or more from your first. Again, find prominent landmarks you can align in a similar way to give your second point of reference, remembering that both reference points need to be aligned at the same time. In theory, next time you are in the area you can swim until you can align all of your reference marks, hopefully putting yourself on the same spot.

The accuracy of your reference marks, their alignment and repeatability, will directly affect the accuracy of your positioning and your ability to find a spot again.

Sometimes a suitable second set of landmarks just isn't available. In that case you can try to find one reference point that interacts both left and right (like lining up the headland and church example) and also vertically up and down, the types of landmarks that work the best for this are objects separated by distance that you can align as if you were lining up sights on a rifle. This could be as simple as lining up roof lines with the horizon or similar. Doing this allows you to both account for left and right position as well as accounting for the distance out from shore.

Of course, all these tricks can also be used in combination with understanding the depths and tides to help put you on the right spot first try.

Picking and using suitable marks takes some practice so try it on some features you don't really need landmarks to find to see how accurate you can make it, and don't forget to note down your marks or even draw a diagram of the sight lines as soon after your dive as you can. Its always frustrating to return to a dive spot only to be unable to recall which house, hill or crack you lined up.

Sun Rise and Set times.

These are pretty obvious figures, easily obtained with a quick google search, or you could even treat yourself by getting out there to see it for yourself, but what do they mean to diving and fish life?

Many plants, algae's and similar, seaweeds included, are affected by the hours of sunlight in the day, with different durations and sun positions encouraging different stages of growth and development. This of course affects the marine life that use them for food and shelter. Coupled with this, many species feed, rest or change their behavior depending on the light levels, hours of darkness and similar. Dawn and dusk diving are often a special treat and offer chances to see species that are rarely seen during the day. Keeping a log of how sites perform at different times of day will help build a picture of how sun position might be affecting fish behavior.

Moon Phases.

Much has been written about the various moon phases and their potential effects on fish behavior, mostly by the angling community. Some swear by fishing at certain points in the Luna calendar, others dismiss it completely. However, it is safe to say that many animals have behaviors linked to moon phases and fish may be no different, not only that but the Moon has a well-documented relationship with the tides. The Moon phase on any day is easily found with a google search, along with in depth explanations about the different Moon phases, but they can be summarised as below:

The Moons phases come from the cycle of the Moons visibility on earth. New

Moon, full Moon, first quarter, third quarter and the phases in between them.

A new Moon occurs when the Moon, Earth and Sun, are in approximate alignment with the Moon situated between the Earth and Sun, thus the illuminated portion of the Moon faces away from Earth and is not visible.

A full Moon occurs when the Earth, Moon and Sun, approximately align but with the moon on the opposite side of Earth to the sun so that the illuminated portion faces Earth and is visible.

The first and third quarter Moons (both appear as 'half-moons') happen when the moon is at a 90-degree angle in respect to the Earth and Sun.

Once you understand the four key phases the phases between can be more easily understood. The periods between the four main phases is defined with four words; crescent, gibbous, waxing and waning. 'Crescent' refers to phases where the Moon is less than half illuminated. 'Gibbous' refers to phrases where its more than half illuminated. 'Waxing' simply means growing, or expanding in illumination, therefore moving towards a full Moon, and 'Waning' means shrinking, or decreasing in illumination, moving towards a new Moon.

Once you have all the terms combining two of the descriptive words will create an accurate Moon phase name. For example, in the completed table above, 'waxing crescent' means; after a new Moon, with the illuminated portion increasing but less than half illuminated.

Whether you need to know the moon phases inside out is debatable but considering them as part of your dive plans, and knowing what phases will be coming next could be an important puzzle piece for some spots.

Weather.

Weather needs no introduction to the seasoned spearfisherman, but undoubtedly has an effect on fish life as well as the obvious impact on conditions for the diver. Whilst the weather on the day, or during your dive is obvious it might also be worth considering the weather for the days immediately before and after your dive. For example, was the day the first settled one after a run of storms or similar. Weather has an ongoing and continuously changing effect on marine life so behaviors you may witness on any given day might be as a result of that day's weather or equally likely due to the prevailing conditions over recent days.

Barometric pressure.

Coupled with weather comes barometric pressure, also referred to as atmospheric pressure. Like moon phases it is much discussed especially in angling circles about its potential impact on fish life and behavior. General consensus seems to be that periods of change in barometric pressure produce more fish than long settled periods.

Generally speaking periods of high pressure are associated with fair weather and low pressure with unsettled weather, barometric pressure figures are included in most weather reports and apps, taking a look a day or two forward and backwards will let you see the general trend which can also be recorded, and is probably a more important indicator than the specific pressure on any given day.

Water temperature.

Water temperature has a very obvious effect on fish. Depending where you are in the world different species will only appear once water temperatures reach certain levels, and changes in temperature are known to trigger other events such as feeding and spawning. Water temperatures are harder to come by than the normal weather data, but a search for local ocean or coastal monitoring buoys will often produce the data. There are also dedicated websites, often aimed at other watersports such as surfing that might give accurate information. Of course, many dive computers and watches now also give instant temperature readings. Due to its massive size, and mass the temperatures of the ocean take a long time to change overall, but there can be relatively big local variations in temperature which generally can't be identified without taking measurements in the water. For example, areas with high tidal flow, rivers or estuaries and similar may have lower than the average temperatures, conversely sheltered shallow bays may see local temperatures above the local average.

Water of different temperatures, doesn't mix perfectly often resulting in thermoclines, which can sometimes be seen as a hazy line in the water, normally with warmer water on top and cooler below. Cooler water, as a general rule, carries more nutrients and therefore potential food, making thermoclines a likely spot for finding fish.

Tides and Currents.

Tides and currents are both important to fish behavior, and diver safety. They are something that most, if not all, spearfishermen have a deeper understanding of compared to many of the other factors included here.

Tidal changes, flow and currents often bring changes to fish behavior, with species becoming more or less active on current and or tidal changes. Currents and tides, especially rising tides or those currents bringing water in from off shore or deeper water, often bring food to marine life, increasing the feeding activities of many species. The same can be said near river mouths, estuaries and places water from the land enters the sea, this fresh water often brings food and nutrients to an area concentrating marine life.

Depending on the location and the species knowing what the currents and tides are doing, direction they are flowing and similar can help you pin point locations to look for fish as well as helping you decide how best to approach them. Many species can be found facing into the current, with more pelagic fish often found actively feeding, especially around current bottlenecks or changes.

Species/Catch Report.

We all need a space to brag about that big fish, but more important than recording your catch could be recording what you saw, including the ones that got away. When reviewing your records knowing which days had the most fish seen, or when and where a particular species was found, even if you didn't manage to catch one, might be invaluable in identifying the correct conditions to find them again.

Fish Behavior/Notes.

As well as recording what was seen or caught also consider what the marine life was doing. Were fish hiding in caves or wrecks, were they feeding, patrolling the weed edges, were they found at depth or in the shallows? On the face of it this might not seem as important as what fish were seen or caught, but knowing where fish are likely to be found and what they are likely to be doing for any given set of conditions will allow you to tailor your technique and hunting style to the conditions and hopefully reduce the time spent trying to find fish on every dive.

Maps.

Finally, there is a space for maps. You could sketch in an overview of the dive site with important features marked, or draw in your landmarks for positioning yourself on a particular feature, even note where you can park and change. Whatever you include make sure it's well labelled and clear, especially for those sites that you don't dive as often. There is nothing worse than looking back for information on an infrequent spot only to find you can't remember, or tell, what your sketch is meant to show or which way its orientated.

Hopefully this brief overview has given you an idea of how to use the Ultimate Spearfishing Almanac to record your dives and improve your understanding of the various factors and conditions that might affect each dive spot. The overriding message should be to record as much information as possible, in a way you will understand it when looking back months, or even years in the future.

Building an accurate picture of a particular spot and how it behaves in a variety of conditions can take a long time but the more often you dive, and the better your records the more chance you have of identifying the combination of factors for any given spot, or species, that give you the greatest chances of success.

DIVE LOG RECORD FORMS

Location:			Coordinates/Mark:				
Date:		Start Time:		Finish Time:			
Sun Rise:		Sun Set:		Moon Phase:			
Conditions							
Overcast	Clear	Sunny	Intermittent	Raining	Storm		
Air Temp	Wind Speed	Wind Direction	Barometric press	Rising	Falling		
Water Conditions							
	Visibility		Water Temp		Wave Height		
Depth/s							
	Tidal State		Low Tide		High Tide		
Current							
Species Seen / Catch Report					Fish Behavior / Notes		

Buy some cheap plastic or swim shoes to save your booties walking to dive spots.

Notes

Map

Location:			Coordinates/Mark:			
Date:		Start Time:		Finish Time:		
Sun Rise:		Sun Set:		Moon Phase:		
Conditions						
Overcast	Clear	Sunny	Intermittent	Raining	Storm	
Air Temp	Wind Speed	Wind Direction	Barometric press	Rising	Falling	
Water Conditions						
Depth/s		Visibility	Water Temp		Wave Height	
Current		Tidal State	Low Tide		High Tide	
Species Seen / Catch Report			Fish Behavior / Notes			

Bleed fish straight away by cutting the gills.

Notes

Map

Location:			Coordinates/Mark:			
Date:		Start Time:		Finish Time:		
Sun Rise:		Sun Set:		Moon Phase:		
Conditions						
Overcast	Clear	Sunny	Intermittent	Raining	Storm	
Air Temp	Wind Speed	Wind Direction	Barometric press	Rising	Falling	
Water Conditions						
Depth/s	Visibility	Water Temp	Wave Height			
Current	Tidal State	Low Tide	High Tide			
Species Seen / Catch Report			Fish Behavior / Notes			

Avoid eye contact with fish while hunting.

Notes

Map

Location:		Coordinates/Mark:			
Date:	Start Time:		Finish Time:		
Sun Rise:	Sun Set:		Moon Phase:		
Conditions					
Overcast	Clear	Sunny	Intermittent	Raining	Storm
Air Temp	Wind Speed	Wind Direction	Barometric press	Rising	Falling
Water Conditions					
Depth/s	Visibility	Tidal State	Water Temp	Wave Height	
Current		Low Tide		High Tide	
Species Seen / Catch Report				Fish Behavior / Notes	

Check a spear for straightness by rolling on a flat surface.

Notes

Map

Location:			Coordinates/Mark:			
Date:		Start Time:		Finish Time:		
Sun Rise:		Sun Set:		Moon Phase:		
Conditions						
Overcast	Clear	Sunny	Intermittent	Raining	Storm	
Air Temp	Wind Speed	Wind Direction	Barometric press	Rising	Falling	
Water Conditions						
Depth/s		Visibility	Water Temp	Wave Height		
Current		Tidal State	Low Tide	High Tide		
Species Seen / Catch Report				Fish Behavior / Notes		

Practice dropping your weight belt regularly.

Notes

Map

Location:			Coordinates/Mark:		
Date:		Start Time:		Finish Time:	
Sun Rise:		Sun Set:		Moon Phase:	
Conditions					
Overcast	Clear	Sunny	Intermittent	Raining	Storm
Air Temp	Wind Speed	Wind Direction	Barometric press	Rising	Falling
Water Conditions					
Depth/s	Visibility	Tidal State	Water Temp	Wave Height	
Current		Low Tide	High Tide		
Species Seen / Catch Report			**Fish Behavior / Notes**		

Check your flopper deploys properly and locks out. They are easy to adjust if needed.

Notes

Map

Location:				Coordinates/Mark:		
Date:		Start Time:		Finish Time:		
Sun Rise:		Sun Set:		Moon Phase:		
Conditions						
Overcast	Clear	Sunny	Intermittent	Raining	Storm	
Air Temp	Wind Speed	Wind Direction	Barometric press	Rising	Falling	
Water Conditions						
Depth/s	Visibility	Water Temp	Wave Height			
Current	Tidal State	Low Tide	High Tide			
Species Seen / Catch Report				Fish Behavior / Notes		

Spend the time, and money, to find a well-fitting wetsuit and mask.

Notes

Map

Location:			Coordinates/Mark:				
Date:		Start Time:		Finish Time:			
Sun Rise:		Sun Set:		Moon Phase:			
Conditions							
Overcast	Clear	Sunny	Intermittent	Raining	Storm		
Air Temp	Wind Speed	Wind Direction	Barometric press	Rising	Falling		
Water Conditions							
Depth/s	Visibility	Water Temp	Wave Height				
Current	Tidal State	Low Tide	High Tide				
Species Seen / Catch Report					Fish Behavior / Notes		

Always tell someone where you are going and your expected return time.

Notes

Map

Location:		Coordinates/Mark:				
Date:		Start Time:		Finish Time:		
Sun Rise:		Sun Set:		Moon Phase:		
Conditions						
Overcast	Clear	Sunny	Intermittent	Raining	Storm	
Air Temp	Wind Speed	Wind Direction	Barometric press	Rising	Falling	
Water Conditions						
Depth/s	Visibility	Tidal State	Water Temp	Wave Height		
Current			Low Tide	High Tide		
Species Seen / Catch Report				Fish Behavior / Notes		

Check local regulations before diving a new area.

Notes

Map

Location:		Coordinates/Mark:				
Date:		Start Time:		Finish Time:		
Sun Rise:		Sun Set:		Moon Phase:		
Conditions						
Overcast	Clear	Sunny	Intermittent	Raining	Storm	
Air Temp	Wind Speed	Wind Direction	Barometric press	Rising	Falling	
Water Conditions						
Depth/s	Visibility	Water Temp		Wave Height		
Current	Tidal State	Low Tide		High Tide		
Species Seen / Catch Report				Fish Behavior / Notes		

Make time to dive without the speargun and focus on technique and getting close to fish.

Notes

Map

Location:			Coordinates/Mark:			
Date:		Start Time:		Finish Time:		
Sun Rise:		Sun Set:		Moon Phase:		
Conditions						
Overcast	Clear	Sunny	Intermittent	Raining	Storm	
Air Temp	Wind Speed	Wind Direction	Barometric press	Rising	Falling	
Water Conditions						
Depth/s	Visibility		Water Temp	Wave Height		
Current	Tidal State		Low Tide	High Tide		
Species Seen / Catch Report				Fish Behavior / Notes		

Fish can be scared by splashing or the noise of a snorkel being cleared.

Notes

Map

Location:			Coordinates/Mark:			
Date:		Start Time:		Finish Time:		
Sun Rise:		Sun Set:		Moon Phase:		
Conditions						
Overcast	Clear	Sunny	Intermittent	Raining	Storm	
Air Temp	Wind Speed	Wind Direction	Barometric press	Rising	Falling	
Water Conditions						
Depth/s	Visibility	Tidal State	Water Temp	Wave Height		
Current			Low Tide	High Tide		
Species Seen / Catch Report				Fish Behavior / Notes		

Keep fish fresh in a slurry of ice and sea water.

Notes
Map

Location:				Coordinates/Mark:			
Date:			Start Time:		Finish Time:		
Sun Rise:			Sun Set:		Moon Phase:		
Conditions							
Overcast		Clear		Sunny		Intermittent	Raining	Storm
Air Temp		Wind Speed		Wind Direction		Barometric press	Rising	Falling
Water Conditions							
Depth/s			Visibility		Water Temp		Wave Height
Current			Tidal State		Low Tide		High Tide
Species Seen / Catch Report						Fish Behavior / Notes	

When on the bottom always try to hide in or behind structure or weed.

Notes

Map

Location:			Coordinates/Mark:		
Date:		Start Time:		Finish Time:	
Sun Rise:		Sun Set:		Moon Phase:	
Conditions					
Overcast	Clear	Sunny	Intermittent	Raining	Storm
Air Temp	Wind Speed	Wind Direction	Barometric press	Rising	Falling
Water Conditions					
Depth/s	Visibility	Water Temp	Wave Height		
Current	Tidal State	Low Tide	High Tide		
Species Seen / Catch Report			Fish Behavior / Notes		

Always dive with a buddy.

Notes

Map

Location:			Coordinates/Mark:				
Date:		Start Time:		Finish Time:			
Sun Rise:		Sun Set:		Moon Phase:			
Conditions							
Overcast	Clear	Sunny	Intermittent	Raining	Storm		
Air Temp	Wind Speed	Wind Direction	Barometric press	Rising	Falling		
Water Conditions							
Depth/s		Visibility		Water Temp	Wave Height		
Current		Tidal State		Low Tide	High Tide		
Species Seen / Catch Report					Fish Behavior / Notes		

Misting up of new masks can be reduced by heating the inside of the lens with a lighter.

Notes

Map

Location:		Coordinates/Mark:			
Date:		Start Time:		Finish Time:	
Sun Rise:		Sun Set:		Moon Phase:	
Conditions					
Overcast	Clear	Sunny	Intermittent	Raining	Storm
Air Temp	Wind Speed	Wind Direction	Barometric press	Rising	Falling
Water Conditions					
	Visibility		Water Temp	Wave Height	
Depth/s					
	Tidal State		Low Tide	High Tide	
Current					

Species Seen / Catch Report	Fish Behavior / Notes

When boat diving, agree a signal to be picked up before starting to dive.

Notes

Map

The Ultimate Spearfishing Almanac

Location:			Coordinates/Mark:	
Date:		Start Time:		Finish Time:
Sun Rise:		Sun Set:		Moon Phase:

Conditions

Overcast	Clear	Sunny	Intermittent	Raining	Storm
Air Temp	Wind Speed	Wind Direction	Barometric press	Rising	Falling

Water Conditions

Depth/s	Visibility	Water Temp	Wave Height
Current	Tidal State	Low Tide	High Tide

Species Seen / Catch Report

Fish Behavior / Notes

Always string your fish before removing the spear.

Notes

Map

Location:		Coordinates/Mark:				
Date:		Start Time:		Finish Time:		
Sun Rise:		Sun Set:		Moon Phase:		
Conditions						
Overcast	Clear	Sunny	Intermittent	Raining	Storm	
Air Temp	Wind Speed	Wind Direction	Barometric press	Rising	Falling	
Water Conditions						
Depth/s	Visibility	Tidal State	Water Temp	Wave Height		
Current			Low Tide	High Tide		
Species Seen / Catch Report				Fish Behavior / Notes		

Tuck your chin into your chest as you descend rather than looking down.

Notes

Map

Location:			Coordinates/Mark:				
Date:		Start Time:		Finish Time:			
Sun Rise:		Sun Set:		Moon Phase:			
Conditions							
Overcast	Clear	Sunny	Intermittent	Raining	Storm		
Air Temp	Wind Speed	Wind Direction	Barometric press	Rising	Falling		
Water Conditions							
Depth/s	Visibility	Water Temp	Wave Height				
Current	Tidal State	Low Tide	High Tide				
Species Seen / Catch Report				Fish Behavior / Notes			

Save fish guts and trimmings to use as burley.

Notes

Map

Location:		Coordinates/Mark:		
Date:	Start Time:	Finish Time:		
Sun Rise:	Sun Set:	Moon Phase:		

Conditions

Overcast	Clear	Sunny	Intermittent	Raining	Storm
Air Temp	Wind Speed	Wind Direction	Barometric press	Rising	Falling

Water Conditions

Depth/s		Visibility	Water Temp	Wave Height	
Current		Tidal State	Low Tide	High Tide	

Species Seen / Catch Report

Fish Behavior / Notes

Remember to flush dive gear with fresh water after use.

Notes

Map

Location:			Coordinates/Mark:				
Date:		Start Time:		Finish Time:			
Sun Rise:		Sun Set:		Moon Phase:			
Conditions							
Overcast	Clear	Sunny	Intermittent	Raining	Storm		
Air Temp	Wind Speed	Wind Direction	Barometric press	Rising	Falling		
Water Conditions							
Depth/s	Visibility	Water Temp		Wave Height			
Current	Tidal State	Low Tide		High Tide			
Species Seen / Catch Report				Fish Behavior / Notes			

Fish generally don't like rapid movements. Stay still and let the fish come to you.

Notes

Map

Location:			Coordinates/Mark:			
Date:		Start Time:		Finish Time:		
Sun Rise:		Sun Set:		Moon Phase:		

Conditions

Overcast	Clear	Sunny	Intermittent	Raining	Storm	
Air Temp	Wind Speed	Wind Direction	Barometric press	Rising	Falling	

Water Conditions

Depth/s	Visibility	Water Temp	Wave Height	
Current	Tidal State	Low Tide	High Tide	

Species Seen / Catch Report

Fish Behavior / Notes

Fin pockets can be adjusted slightly by softening with hot water or air.

Notes

Map

Location:		Coordinates/Mark:				
Date:		Start Time:		Finish Time:		
Sun Rise:		Sun Set:		Moon Phase:		
Conditions						
Overcast	Clear	Sunny	Intermittent	Raining	Storm	
Air Temp	Wind Speed	Wind Direction	Barometric press	Rising	Falling	
Water Conditions						
Depth/s		Visibility		Water Temp	Wave Height	
Current		Tidal State		Low Tide	High Tide	
Species Seen / Catch Report				Fish Behavior / Notes		

Repair minor nicks in wetsuits before they become tears.

Notes

Map

Location:				Coordinates/Mark:			
Date:		Start Time:			Finish Time:		
Sun Rise:		Sun Set:			Moon Phase:		
Conditions							
Overcast	Clear	Sunny	Intermittent		Raining	Storm	
Air Temp	Wind Speed	Wind Direction	Barometric press		Rising	Falling	
Water Conditions							
Depth/s		Visibility		Water Temp		Wave Height	
Current		Tidal State		Low Tide		High Tide	
Species Seen / Catch Report						Fish Behavior / Notes	

Keep your dive knife where it can be reached by either hand.

Notes

Map

Location:				Coordinates/Mark:			
Date:		Start Time:		Finish Time:			
Sun Rise:		Sun Set:		Moon Phase:			
Conditions							
Overcast	Clear	Sunny	Intermittent	Raining	Storm		
Air Temp	Wind Speed	Wind Direction	Barometric press	Rising	Falling		
Water Conditions							
Depth/s	Visibility	Water Temp	Wave Height				
Current	Tidal State	Low Tide	High Tide				
Species Seen / Catch Report				Fish Behavior / Notes			

Fish are often found facing into the current.

Notes

Map

Location:			Coordinates/Mark:			
Date:		Start Time:		Finish Time:		
Sun Rise:		Sun Set:		Moon Phase:		
Conditions						
Overcast	Clear	Sunny	Intermittent	Raining	Storm	
Air Temp	Wind Speed	Wind Direction	Barometric press	Rising	Falling	
Water Conditions						
Depth/s	Visibility	Tidal State	Water Temp	Wave Height		
Current		Low Tide		High Tide		
Species Seen / Catch Report				**Fish Behavior / Notes**		

Remember to look behind you occasionally as well as ahead.

Notes

Map

Location:			Coordinates/Mark:				
Date:		Start Time:		Finish Time:			
Sun Rise:		Sun Set:		Moon Phase:			
Conditions							
Overcast	Clear	Sunny	Intermittent	Raining	Storm		
Air Temp	Wind Speed	Wind Direction	Barometric press	Rising	Falling		
Water Conditions							
Depth/s		Visibility	Water Temp	Wave Height			
Current		Tidal State	Low Tide	High Tide			
Species Seen / Catch Report				Fish Behavior / Notes			

Some fish respond to noises like grunting or scraping rocks.

Notes

Map

Location:			Coordinates/Mark:			
Date:		Start Time:		Finish Time:		
Sun Rise:		Sun Set:		Moon Phase:		
Conditions						
Overcast	Clear	Sunny	Intermittent	Raining	Storm	
Air Temp	Wind Speed	Wind Direction	Barometric press	Rising	Falling	
Water Conditions						
Depth/s	Visibility		Water Temp	Wave Height		
Current	Tidal State		Low Tide	High Tide		
Species Seen / Catch Report					Fish Behavior / Notes	

Never push your limits, always maintain a long enough recovery period between dives.

Notes

Map

Location:			Coordinates/Mark:			
Date:		Start Time:		Finish Time:		
Sun Rise:		Sun Set:		Moon Phase:		

Conditions

Overcast	Clear	Sunny	Intermittent	Raining	Storm	
Air Temp	Wind Speed	Wind Direction	Barometric press	Rising	Falling	

Water Conditions

Depth/s	Visibility	Water Temp	Wave Height	
Current	Tidal State	Low Tide	High Tide	

Species Seen / Catch Report

Fish Behavior / Notes

Keep your dive knife sharp, try cutting some spare float or spear line to check.

Notes

Map

Location:				Coordinates/Mark:			
Date:			Start Time:		Finish Time:		
Sun Rise:			Sun Set:		Moon Phase:		
Conditions							
Overcast	Clear		Sunny	Intermittent	Raining	Storm	
Air Temp	Wind Speed		Wind Direction	Barometric press	Rising	Falling	
Water Conditions							
Depth/s		Visibility		Water Temp		Wave Height	
Current		Tidal State		Low Tide	High Tide		
Species Seen / Catch Report				Fish Behavior / Notes			

Check your speargun line, crimps and swivels before every trip.

Notes

Map

Location:			Coordinates/Mark:			
Date:		Start Time:		Finish Time:		
Sun Rise:		Sun Set:		Moon Phase:		
Conditions						
Overcast	Clear	Sunny	Intermittent	Raining	Storm	
Air Temp	Wind Speed	Wind Direction	Barometric press	Rising	Falling	
Water Conditions						
Depth/s	Visibility	Tidal State	Water Temp	Low Tide	Wave Height	High Tide
Species Seen / Catch Report				Fish Behavior / Notes		

Don't inhale to full capacity during your breath up, only on the final breath.

Notes

Map

Location:		Coordinates/Mark:				
Date:		Start Time:		Finish Time:		
Sun Rise:		Sun Set:		Moon Phase:		
Conditions						
Overcast	Clear	Sunny	Intermittent	Raining	Storm	
Air Temp	Wind Speed	Wind Direction	Barometric press	Rising	Falling	
Water Conditions						
Depth/s		Visibility	Water Temp	Wave Height		
Current		Tidal State	Low Tide	High Tide		
Species Seen / Catch Report				Fish Behavior / Notes		

Fish can sometimes be attracted by throwing sand from the bottom.

Notes

Map

Location:		Coordinates/Mark:			
Date:		Start Time:		Finish Time:	
Sun Rise:		Sun Set:		Moon Phase:	
Conditions					
Overcast	Clear	Sunny	Intermittent	Raining	Storm
Air Temp	Wind Speed	Wind Direction	Barometric press	Rising	Falling
Water Conditions					
Depth/s	Visibility	Water Temp		Wave Height	
Current	Tidal State	Low Tide		High Tide	
Species Seen / Catch Report			Fish Behavior / Notes		

Spend time observing the water before getting in at a new site.

| Notes |
| Map |

Location:				Coordinates/Mark:			
Date:		Start Time:				Finish Time:	
Sun Rise:		Sun Set:				Moon Phase:	
Conditions							
Overcast	Clear	Sunny	Intermittent	Raining	Storm		
Air Temp	Wind Speed	Wind Direction	Barometric press	Rising	Falling		
Water Conditions							
Depth/s	Visibility	Tidal State	Water Temp		Wave Height		
Current		Low Tide		High Tide			
Species Seen / Catch Report				Fish Behavior / Notes			

Keep your spear sharp, and straight!

Notes

Map

Location:			Coordinates/Mark:			
Date:		Start Time:		Finish Time:		
Sun Rise:		Sun Set:		Moon Phase:		
Conditions						
Overcast	Clear	Sunny	Intermittent	Raining	Storm	
Air Temp	Wind Speed	Wind Direction	Barometric press	Rising	Falling	
Water Conditions						
Depth/s	Visibility	Tidal State	Water Temp	Wave Height		
Current			Low Tide	High Tide		
Species Seen / Catch Report				Fish Behavior / Notes		

Fish in poor visibility tend to be more easily spooked.

Notes

Map

Location:				Coordinates/Mark:			
Date:		Start Time:			Finish Time:		
Sun Rise:		Sun Set:			Moon Phase:		
Conditions							
Overcast	Clear	Sunny	Intermittent	Raining	Storm		
Air Temp	Wind Speed	Wind Direction	Barometric press	Rising	Falling		
Water Conditions							
Depth/s	Visibility	Water Temp		Wave Height			
Current	Tidal State	Low Tide		High Tide			
Species Seen / Catch Report				Fish Behavior / Notes			

Always use a dive float with a large diver down flag.

Notes

Map

Location:			Coordinates/Mark:			
Date:		Start Time:		Finish Time:		
Sun Rise:		Sun Set:		Moon Phase:		
Conditions						
Overcast	Clear	Sunny	Intermittent	Raining	Storm	
Air Temp	Wind Speed	Wind Direction	Barometric press	Rising	Falling	
Water Conditions						
Depth/s	Visibility	Water Temp		Wave Height		
Current		Tidal State	Low Tide	High Tide		
Species Seen / Catch Report				Fish Behavior / Notes		

A handful of change or silver foil can be thrown as a makeshift flasher.

Notes

Map

Location:			Coordinates/Mark:			
Date:		Start Time:		Finish Time:		
Sun Rise:		Sun Set:		Moon Phase:		
Conditions						
Overcast	Clear	Sunny	Intermittent	Raining	Storm	
Air Temp	Wind Speed	Wind Direction	Barometric press	Rising	Falling	
Water Conditions						
Depth/s		Visibility	Water Temp	Wave Height		
Current		Tidal State	Low Tide	High Tide		
Species Seen / Catch Report				**Fish Behavior / Notes**		

Good quality float line should hardly tangle.

Notes

Map

Location:		Coordinates/Mark:			
Date:		Start Time:		Finish Time:	
Sun Rise:		Sun Set:		Moon Phase:	
Conditions					
Overcast	Clear	Sunny	Intermittent	Raining	Storm
Air Temp	Wind Speed	Wind Direction	Barometric press	Rising	Falling
Water Conditions					
Depth/s	Visibility		Water Temp	Wave Height	
Current	Tidal State		Low Tide	High Tide	
Species Seen / Catch Report			Fish Behavior / Notes		

Wash fish in sea water where possible it helps preserve flavor.

Notes

Map

Location:				Coordinates/Mark:			
Date:			Start Time:		Finish Time:		
Sun Rise:			Sun Set:		Moon Phase:		
Conditions							
Overcast		Clear		Sunny	Intermittent	Raining	Storm
Air Temp		Wind Speed		Wind Direction	Barometric press	Rising	Falling
Water Conditions							
Depth/s		Visibility		Water Temp		Wave Height	
Current		Tidal State		Low Tide		High Tide	
Species Seen / Catch Report				Fish Behavior / Notes			

Don't put oil or grease in your trigger mechanism just keep it clean and regularly flushed.

Notes

Map

The Ultimate Spearfishing Almanac

Location:		Coordinates/Mark:			
Date:		Start Time:		Finish Time:	
Sun Rise:		Sun Set:		Moon Phase:	
Conditions					
Overcast	Clear	Sunny	Intermittent	Raining	Storm
Air Temp	Wind Speed	Wind Direction	Barometric press	Rising	Falling
Water Conditions					
Depth/s		Visibility	Water Temp	Wave Height	
Current		Tidal State	Low Tide	High Tide	
Species Seen / Catch Report			**Fish Behavior / Notes**		

Remove your snorkel before you dive. Its quieter, and makes resuscitation easier if required.

Notes

Map

Location:		Coordinates/Mark:		
Date:	Start Time:		Finish Time:	
Sun Rise:	Sun Set:		Moon Phase:	
Conditions				
Overcast	Clear	Sunny	Intermittent	Raining	Storm
Air Temp	Wind Speed	Wind Direction	Barometric press	Rising	Falling
Water Conditions				
Depth/s	Visibility		Water Temp	Wave Height
	Current	Tidal State	Low Tide	High Tide
Species Seen / Catch Report			**Fish Behavior / Notes**	

Remember to check holes, cracks and caves, fish can hide in surprisingly small places.

Notes

Map

Location:			Coordinates/Mark:			
Date:		Start Time:		Finish Time:		
Sun Rise:		Sun Set:		Moon Phase:		
Conditions						
Overcast	Clear	Sunny	Intermittent	Raining	Storm	
Air Temp	Wind Speed	Wind Direction	Barometric press	Rising	Falling	
Water Conditions						
Depth/s	Visibility	Water Temp	Wave Height			
Current	Tidal State	Low Tide	High Tide			
Species Seen / Catch Report			Fish Behavior / Notes			

Gut fish as soon as possible after catching.

Notes

Map

Location:			Coordinates/Mark:			
Date:		Start Time:		Finish Time:		
Sun Rise:		Sun Set:		Moon Phase:		
Conditions						
Overcast	Clear	Sunny	Intermittent	Raining	Storm	
Air Temp	Wind Speed	Wind Direction	Barometric press	Rising	Falling	
Water Conditions						
Depth/s	Visibility	Tidal State	Water Temp	Wave Height		
Current			Low Tide	High Tide		
Species Seen / Catch Report				Fish Behavior / Notes		

A lure or muppet at the end of your speargun can bring fish closer.

Notes

Map

The Ultimate Spearfishing Almanac

Location:			Coordinates/Mark:			
Date:		Start Time:		Finish Time:		
Sun Rise:		Sun Set:		Moon Phase:		
Conditions						
Overcast	Clear	Sunny	Intermittent	Raining	Storm	
Air Temp	Wind Speed	Wind Direction	Barometric press	Rising	Falling	
Water Conditions						
Depth/s		Visibility	Water Temp	Wave Height		
Current		Tidal State	Low Tide	High Tide		
Species Seen / Catch Report				**Fish Behavior / Notes**		

Never point a loaded gun at anyone, especially your buddy.

Notes

Map

Location:				Coordinates/Mark:			
Date:			Start Time:		Finish Time:		
Sun Rise:			Sun Set:		Moon Phase:		
Conditions							
Overcast	Clear		Sunny	Intermittent	Raining	Storm	
Air Temp	Wind Speed		Wind Direction	Barometric press	Rising	Falling	
Water Conditions							
Depth/s		Visibility		Water Temp		Wave Height	
Current		Tidal State		Low Tide		High Tide	
Species Seen / Catch Report				Fish Behavior / Notes			

Many fish have spines, learn which and where!

Notes

Map

Location:				Coordinates/Mark:			
Date:		Start Time:			Finish Time:		
Sun Rise:		Sun Set:			Moon Phase:		
Conditions							
Overcast	Clear	Sunny	Intermittent	Raining	Storm		
Air Temp	Wind Speed	Wind Direction	Barometric press	Rising	Falling		
Water Conditions							
Depth/s		Visibility		Water Temp	Wave Height		
Current		Tidal State		Low Tide	High Tide		
Species Seen / Catch Report						Fish Behavior / Notes	

Always lube up your wetsuit.

Notes
Map

Location:		Coordinates/Mark:					
Date:		Start Time:		Finish Time:			
Sun Rise:		Sun Set:		Moon Phase:			
Conditions							
Overcast	Clear	Sunny	Intermittent	Raining	Storm		
Air Temp	Wind Speed	Wind Direction	Barometric press	Rising	Falling		
Water Conditions							
Depth/s	Visibility	Tidal State	Water Temp	Wave Height			
Current			Low Tide	High Tide			
Species Seen / Catch Report				Fish Behavior / Notes			

If you can't equalise fully don't dive. Pain is not normal.

Notes

Map

Location:			Coordinates/Mark:			
Date:		Start Time:		Finish Time:		
Sun Rise:		Sun Set:		Moon Phase:		
Conditions						
Overcast	Clear	Sunny	Intermittent	Raining	Storm	
Air Temp	Wind Speed	Wind Direction	Barometric press	Rising	Falling	
Water Conditions						
Depth/s	Visibility		Water Temp	Wave Height		
	Current	Tidal State	Low Tide	High Tide		
Species Seen / Catch Report				Fish Behavior / Notes		

Always take some water with you, dehydration will ruin your dive.

Notes

Map

Location:			Coordinates/Mark:			
Date:		Start Time:		Finish Time:		
Sun Rise:		Sun Set:		Moon Phase:		
Conditions						
Overcast	Clear	Sunny	Intermittent	Raining	Storm	
Air Temp	Wind Speed	Wind Direction	Barometric press	Rising	Falling	
Water Conditions						
Depth/s	Visibility	Tidal State	Water Temp	Wave Height		
Current		Low Tide	High Tide			
Species Seen / Catch Report			**Fish Behavior / Notes**			

Try new locations, times or tides. Don't get stuck doing the same dive over and over.

Notes

Map

Location:		Coordinates/Mark:			
Date:		Start Time:		Finish Time:	
Sun Rise:		Sun Set:		Moon Phase:	
Conditions					
Overcast	Clear	Sunny	Intermittent	Raining	Storm
Air Temp	Wind Speed	Wind Direction	Barometric press	Rising	Falling
Water Conditions					
Depth/s	Visibility	Tidal State	Water Temp	Wave Height	
Current				Low Tide	High Tide
Species Seen / Catch Report			Fish Behavior / Notes		

Keep all your kit in one bag or container, you are less likely to forget something.

Notes

Map

Location:		Coordinates/Mark:		
Date:		Start Time:		Finish Time:
Sun Rise:		Sun Set:		Moon Phase:
Conditions				
Overcast	Clear	Sunny	Intermittent	Raining	Storm
Air Temp	Wind Speed	Wind Direction	Barometric press	Rising	Falling
Water Conditions				
Depth/s		Visibility	Water Temp	Wave Height
Current		Tidal State	Low Tide	High Tide
Species Seen / Catch Report			Fish Behavior / Notes	

Spears can rebound off of rocks. Be careful.

Notes

Map

Location:			Coordinates/Mark:			
Date:		Start Time:		Finish Time:		
Sun Rise:		Sun Set:		Moon Phase:		
Conditions						
Overcast	Clear	Sunny	Intermittent	Raining	Storm	
Air Temp	Wind Speed	Wind Direction	Barometric press	Rising	Falling	
Water Conditions						
Depth/s		Visibility	Water Temp	Wave Height		
Current		Tidal State	Low Tide	High Tide		
Species Seen / Catch Report				Fish Behavior / Notes		

Different fish, and different sizes of fish like different things, explore.

Notes

Map

Location:			Coordinates/Mark:			
Date:		Start Time:		Finish Time:		
Sun Rise:		Sun Set:		Moon Phase:		
Conditions						
Overcast	Clear	Sunny	Intermittent	Raining	Storm	
Air Temp	Wind Speed	Wind Direction	Barometric press	Rising	Falling	
Water Conditions						
Depth/s	Visibility	Tidal State	Water Temp	Wave Height		
Current		Tidal State	Low Tide	High Tide		
Species Seen / Catch Report			**Fish Behavior / Notes**			

Do everything more smoothly and slowly. It will help your diving.

Notes

Map

The Ultimate Spearfishing Almanac

Location:		Coordinates/Mark:		
Date:		Start Time:		Finish Time:
Sun Rise:		Sun Set:		Moon Phase:

Conditions

Overcast	Clear	Sunny	Intermittent	Raining	Storm
Air Temp	Wind Speed	Wind Direction	Barometric press	Rising	Falling

Water Conditions

Depth/s	Visibility	Water Temp	Wave Height	
Current	Tidal State	Low Tide	High Tide	

Species Seen / Catch Report

Fish Behavior / Notes

Staying down longer, or diving deeper probably won't get you more fish.

Notes

Map

Location:				Coordinates/Mark:			
Date:		Start Time:			Finish Time:		
Sun Rise:		Sun Set:			Moon Phase:		
Conditions							
Overcast	Clear	Sunny	Intermittent	Raining	Storm		
Air Temp	Wind Speed	Wind Direction	Barometric press	Rising	Falling		
Water Conditions							
Depth/s	Visibility	Water Temp	Wave Height				
Current	Tidal State	Low Tide	High Tide				
Species Seen / Catch Report				Fish Behavior / Notes			

Changing something on your gun, like bands, spear or muzzle will affect the point of aim.

Notes

Map

Location:			Coordinates/Mark:			
Date:		Start Time:		Finish Time:		
Sun Rise:		Sun Set:		Moon Phase:		
Conditions						
Overcast	Clear	Sunny	Intermittent	Raining	Storm	
Air Temp	Wind Speed	Wind Direction	Barometric press	Rising	Falling	
Water Conditions						
Depth/s	Visibility	Water Temp	Wave Height			
Current	Tidal State	Low Tide	High Tide			
Species Seen / Catch Report			Fish Behavior / Notes			

Boats are great, but will cost many times what you think no matter how good your planning.

Notes

Map

The Ultimate Spearfishing Almanac

Location:		Coordinates/Mark:			
Date:		Start Time:		Finish Time:	
Sun Rise:		Sun Set:		Moon Phase:	
Conditions					
Overcast	Clear	Sunny	Intermittent	Raining	Storm
Air Temp	Wind Speed	Wind Direction	Barometric press	Rising	Falling
Water Conditions					
Depth/s	Visibility		Water Temp	Wave Height	
Current	Tidal State		Low Tide	High Tide	
Species Seen / Catch Report			**Fish Behavior / Notes**		

Never fire a speargun out of the water.

Notes

Map

Location:			Coordinates/Mark:				
Date:		Start Time:		Finish Time:			
Sun Rise:		Sun Set:		Moon Phase:			
Conditions							
Overcast	Clear	Sunny	Intermittent	Raining	Storm		
Air Temp	Wind Speed	Wind Direction	Barometric press	Rising	Falling		
Water Conditions							
Depth/s	Visibility	Tidal State	Water Temp	Wave Height			
Current		Low Tide	High Tide				
Species Seen / Catch Report				Fish Behavior / Notes			

Equalise before you leave the surface, and regularly as you descend.

Notes

Map

Location:			Coordinates/Mark:			
Date:		Start Time:		Finish Time:		
Sun Rise:		Sun Set:		Moon Phase:		
Conditions						
Overcast	Clear	Sunny	Intermittent	Raining	Storm	
Air Temp	Wind Speed	Wind Direction	Barometric press	Rising	Falling	
Water Conditions						
Depth/s		Visibility	Water Temp		Wave Height	
Current		Tidal State	Low Tide		High Tide	
Species Seen / Catch Report					Fish Behavior / Notes	

Masks seal to clean shaven skin best.

Notes

Map

Location:			Coordinates/Mark:		
Date:		Start Time:		Finish Time:	
Sun Rise:		Sun Set:		Moon Phase:	
Conditions					
Overcast	Clear	Sunny	Intermittent	Raining	Storm
Air Temp	Wind Speed	Wind Direction	Barometric press	Rising	Falling
Water Conditions					
Depth/s	Visibility	Water Temp		Wave Height	
Current	Tidal State	Low Tide		High Tide	
Species Seen / Catch Report				Fish Behavior / Notes	

What you have eaten/drunk before diving will affect how you dive.

Notes

Map

Location:			Coordinates/Mark:			
Date:		Start Time:		Finish Time:		
Sun Rise:		Sun Set:		Moon Phase:		
Conditions						
Overcast	Clear	Sunny	Intermittent	Raining	Storm	
Air Temp	Wind Speed	Wind Direction	Barometric press	Rising	Falling	
Water Conditions						
Depth/s	Visibility	Water Temp	Wave Height			
Current	Tidal State	Low Tide	High Tide			
Species Seen / Catch Report			Fish Behavior / Notes			

If you have a beard try Vaseline or a small trim under the nose to help your mask seal.

Notes

Map

Location:		Coordinates/Mark:			
Date:		Start Time:		Finish Time:	
Sun Rise:		Sun Set:		Moon Phase:	
Conditions					
Overcast	Clear	Sunny	Intermittent	Raining	Storm
Air Temp	Wind Speed	Wind Direction	Barometric press	Rising	Falling
Water Conditions					
Depth/s	Visibility	Tidal State	Water Temp	Wave Height	
Current			Low Tide	High Tide	
Species Seen / Catch Report			Fish Behavior / Notes		

Practice shooting regularly, plastic bags or foam cut outs make great targets.

Notes

Map

Location:		Coordinates/Mark:				
Date:		Start Time:		Finish Time:		
Sun Rise:		Sun Set:		Moon Phase:		
Conditions						
Overcast	Clear	Sunny	Intermittent	Raining	Storm	
Air Temp	Wind Speed	Wind Direction	Barometric press	Rising	Falling	
Water Conditions						
Depth/s	Visibility	Water Temp		Wave Height		
Current	Tidal State	Low Tide		High Tide		
Species Seen / Catch Report				Fish Behavior / Notes		

Keeping the sun at your back can help when stalking fish.

Notes

Map

Location:			Coordinates/Mark:			
Date:		Start Time:		Finish Time:		
Sun Rise:		Sun Set:		Moon Phase:		
Conditions						
Overcast	Clear	Sunny	Intermittent	Raining	Storm	
Air Temp	Wind Speed	Wind Direction	Barometric press	Rising	Falling	
Water Conditions						
Depth/s	Visibility		Water Temp		Wave Height	
Current	Tidal State		Low Tide		High Tide	
Species Seen / Catch Report			Fish Behavior / Notes			

Camouflage equipment isn't essential but sometimes can help.

Notes

Map

Location:		Coordinates/Mark:			
Date:		Start Time:		Finish Time:	
Sun Rise:		Sun Set:		Moon Phase:	
Conditions					
Overcast	Clear	Sunny	Intermittent	Raining	Storm
Air Temp	Wind Speed	Wind Direction	Barometric press	Rising	Falling
Water Conditions					
Depth/s	Visibility	Tidal State	Water Temp	Wave Height	
Current			Low Tide	High Tide	
Species Seen / Catch Report			Fish Behavior / Notes		

Be conscious of, and courteous to other water users.

Notes

Map

Location:				Coordinates/Mark:			
Date:				Start Time:		Finish Time:	
Sun Rise:				Sun Set:		Moon Phase:	
Conditions							
Overcast		Clear		Sunny		Intermittent	Raining	Storm
Air Temp		Wind Speed		Wind Direction		Barometric press	Rising	Falling
Water Conditions							
Depth/s				Visibility		Water Temp	Wave Height
Current				Tidal State		Low Tide	High Tide
Species Seen / Catch Report						Fish Behavior / Notes	

Learn the rule of twelfths to help predict currents.

Notes

Map

Location:				Coordinates/Mark:			
Date:		Start Time:			Finish Time:		
Sun Rise:		Sun Set:			Moon Phase:		
Conditions							
Overcast	Clear	Sunny	Intermittent	Raining	Storm		
Air Temp	Wind Speed	Wind Direction	Barometric press	Rising	Falling		
Water Conditions							
Depth/s	Visibility		Water Temp		Wave Height		
Current		Tidal State	Low Tide		High Tide		
Species Seen / Catch Report				Fish Behavior / Notes			

Data from national weather buoys is available online.

Notes

Map

Location:			Coordinates/Mark:			
Date:		Start Time:		Finish Time:		
Sun Rise:		Sun Set:		Moon Phase:		
Conditions						
Overcast	Clear	Sunny	Intermittent	Raining	Storm	
Air Temp	Wind Speed	Wind Direction	Barometric press	Rising	Falling	
Water Conditions						
Depth/s		Visibility	Water Temp		Wave Height	
Current		Tidal State	Low Tide		High Tide	
Species Seen / Catch Report			Fish Behavior / Notes			

Learn to store float lines in a figure eight coil with half hitches for easy use and storage.

Notes

Map

Spearfishing Log

Location:			Coordinates/Mark:			
Date:		Start Time:		Finish Time:		
Sun Rise:		Sun Set:		Moon Phase:		
Conditions						
Overcast	Clear	Sunny	Intermittent	Raining	Storm	
Air Temp	Wind Speed	Wind Direction	Barometric press	Rising	Falling	
Water Conditions						
Depth/s	Visibility		Water Temp		Wave Height	
Current	Tidal State		Low Tide		High Tide	
Species Seen / Catch Report				Fish Behavior / Notes		

A proper fish scaler is faster, and cleaner, than using a knife.

Notes

Map

Location:			Coordinates/Mark:			
Date:		Start Time:		Finish Time:		
Sun Rise:		Sun Set:		Moon Phase:		
Conditions						
Overcast	Clear	Sunny	Intermittent	Raining	Storm	
Air Temp	Wind Speed	Wind Direction	Barometric press	Rising	Falling	
Water Conditions						
Depth/s		Visibility	Water Temp		Wave Height	
Current		Tidal State	Low Tide		High Tide	
Species Seen / Catch Report				**Fish Behavior / Notes**		

152

Invest in a set of scales. Everyone overestimates weights, especially when starting out.

Notes

Map

Location:			Coordinates/Mark:			
Date:		Start Time:		Finish Time:		
Sun Rise:		Sun Set:		Moon Phase:		
Conditions						
Overcast	Clear	Sunny	Intermittent	Raining	Storm	
Air Temp	Wind Speed	Wind Direction	Barometric press	Rising	Falling	
Water Conditions						
Depth/s	Visibility	Tidal State	Water Temp	Wave Height		
Current		Low Tide	High Tide			
Species Seen / Catch Report			Fish Behavior / Notes			

Offshore winds can help to clear the visibility and encourage pelagic hunters.

Notes

Map

The Ultimate Spearfishing Almanac

Location:		Coordinates/Mark:		
Date:		Start Time:	Finish Time:	
Sun Rise:		Sun Set:	Moon Phase:	
Conditions				
Overcast	Clear	Sunny	Intermittent	Raining	Storm
Air Temp	Wind Speed	Wind Direction	Barometric press	Rising	Falling
Water Conditions				
Depth/s	Visibility	Water Temp	Wave Height	
Current	Tidal State	Low Tide	High Tide	
Species Seen / Catch Report			Fish Behavior / Notes	

For maximum relaxation, breath out for at least twice as long as you breath in.

Notes

Map

Location:			Coordinates/Mark:				
Date:		Start Time:		Finish Time:			
Sun Rise:		Sun Set:		Moon Phase:			
Conditions							
Overcast	Clear	Sunny	Intermittent	Raining	Storm		
Air Temp	Wind Speed	Wind Direction	Barometric press	Rising	Falling		
Water Conditions							
Depth/s		Visibility	Water Temp	Wave Height			
	Current	Tidal State	Low Tide	High Tide			
Species Seen / Catch Report				Fish Behavior / Notes			

Consider adding a handheld VHF and or PLB to your dive kit.

Notes

Map

Location:			Coordinates/Mark:			
Date:		Start Time:		Finish Time:		
Sun Rise:		Sun Set:		Moon Phase:		
Conditions						
Overcast	Clear	Sunny	Intermittent	Raining	Storm	
Air Temp	Wind Speed	Wind Direction	Barometric press	Rising	Falling	
Water Conditions						
Depth/s	Visibility	Tidal State	Water Temp	Wave Height		
Current			Low Tide	High Tide		
Species Seen / Catch Report				Fish Behavior / Notes		

Yoga and meditation are proven to be beneficial to freediving and spearfishing.

Notes

Map

Location:		Coordinates/Mark:		
Date:		Start Time:	Finish Time:	
Sun Rise:		Sun Set:	Moon Phase:	
Conditions				
Overcast	Clear	Sunny	Intermittent	Raining	Storm
Air Temp	Wind Speed	Wind Direction	Barometric press	Rising	Falling
Water Conditions				
Depth/s	Visibility	Water Temp		Wave Height
Current	Tidal State	Low Tide		High Tide
Species Seen / Catch Report		Fish Behavior / Notes		

The best training is actually diving but apnea walks and similar can be done on dry land.

Notes

Map

Location:		Coordinates/Mark:			
Date:		Start Time:		Finish Time:	
Sun Rise:		Sun Set:		Moon Phase:	

Conditions

Overcast	Clear	Sunny	Intermittent	Raining	Storm
Air Temp	Wind Speed	Wind Direction	Barometric press	Rising	Falling

Water Conditions

Depth/s	Visibility	Water Temp	Wave Height		
Current	Tidal State	Low Tide	High Tide		

Species Seen / Catch Report | Fish Behavior / Notes

Areas where freshwater flows into the sea can be productive, but often have less visibility.

Notes

Map

Location:		Coordinates/Mark:			
Date:		Start Time:		Finish Time:	
Sun Rise:		Sun Set:		Moon Phase:	
Conditions					
Overcast	Clear	Sunny	Intermittent	Raining	Storm
Air Temp	Wind Speed	Wind Direction	Barometric press	Rising	Falling
Water Conditions					
Visibility		Water Temp		Wave Height	
Depth/s		Tidal State	Low Tide	High Tide	
		Current			
Species Seen / Catch Report			Fish Behavior / Notes		

A torch can be used to look in holes as well as helping if you get caught out after dark.

Notes

Map

Location:			Coordinates/Mark:			
Date:		Start Time:		Finish Time:		
Sun Rise:		Sun Set:		Moon Phase:		
Conditions						
Overcast	Clear	Sunny	Intermittent	Raining	Storm	
Air Temp	Wind Speed	Wind Direction	Barometric press	Rising	Falling	
Water Conditions						
Depth/s		Visibility	Water Temp		Wave Height	
		Tidal State	Low Tide		High Tide	
Current						
Species Seen / Catch Report				Fish Behavior / Notes		

Angling forums and magazines can be a valuable resource for finding potential dive spots.

Notes

Map

Location:			Coordinates/Mark:			
Date:		Start Time:		Finish Time:		
Sun Rise:		Sun Set:		Moon Phase:		
Conditions						
Overcast	Clear	Sunny	Intermittent	Raining	Storm	
Air Temp	Wind Speed	Wind Direction	Barometric press	Rising	Falling	
Water Conditions						
Depth/s	Visibility	Water Temp	Wave Height			
Current	Tidal State	Low Tide	High Tide			
Species Seen / Catch Report			Fish Behavior / Notes			

Always put safety first, no fish, or spot is worth a life.

Notes

Map

TIME TO REVIEW

Now you have detailed records for a number of dives, take the time to look back through each record, highlight the dives that were the most successful and look for trends with any of the conditions you recorded. Did a certain tide or weather condition produce more fish, was it a time of day or a combination of factors? Don't forget to not only consider the fish caught but also the fish seen, and if you are hunting for that personal best take special note of the conditions where the biggest fish were seen, even if you didn't get a shot. The behavior of larger fish is often markedly different to that of younger or smaller fish.

If you have more than one record book make sure to look back over multiple spots or multiple years to build an even more complete picture.

You might find it useful to put some of your observations in a table with dates/dives across the top and observations about conditions, weather and similar down the side. This way you can add a cross, mark, or similar, against each point where it corresponds with a good catch or sighting, ending up with a visual representation of the most frequent conditions or most important observations about the environment and dive site that relate to the best fishing.

There is a blank table included on the next double page spread for you to complete as you wish, with an example of how you might like to complete it below, followed by a few pages for your notes and summary, and don't forget to order yourself a replacement 'Ultimate Spearfishing Almanac' to continue logging information on your future dives.

	12/5	17/5	25/5	8/6	19/6	20/6	21/6	02/7	04/7
RISING TIDE	X		X	X		X	X		
SLACK TIDE		X							
FALLING TIDE					X			X	X
CLEAR		X			X				
OVERCAST	X		X	X		X	X	X	

BLANK TABLE FOR OBSERVATIONS.

NOTES

NOTES

NOTES

Printed in Great Britain
by Amazon